# student WORKBOOK

## A2 US Government & Politics

Re

D1512631

Kay Moxon   **Series Editor:** Eric Ma

Introduction .............................................................................. 2
Elections and voting behaviour ................................................ 3
Political parties ........................................................................ 29
Pressure groups ...................................................................... 40
Racial and ethnic politics ........................................................ 53

Philip Allan Updates, an imprint of Hodder Education, an Hachette UK company, Market Place, Deddington, Oxfordshire OX15 0SE

*Orders*

Bookpoint Ltd, 130 Milton Park, Abingdon, Oxfordshire OX14 4SB

tel: 01235 827720 fax: 01235 400454

e-mail: uk.orders@bookpoint.co.uk

Lines are open 9.00 a.m.–5.00 p.m., Monday to Saturday, with a 24-hour message answering service. You can also order through the Philip Allan Updates website: www.philipallan.co.uk

© Philip Allan Updates 2009

ISBN 978-0-340-99002-5

First printed 2009

Impression number 5 4 3 2 1

Year 2014 2013 2012 2011 2010 2009

All rights reserved; no part of this publication may be reproduced, stored in a retrieval system, or transmitted, in any other form or by any means, electronic, mechanical, photocopying, recording or otherwise without either the prior written permission of Philip Allan Updates or a licence permitting restricted copying in the United Kingdom issued by the Copyright Licensing Agency Ltd, Saffron House, 6–10 Kirby Street, London EC1N 8TS.

Typeset by D.C. Graphic Design, Swanley Village

Printed in Spain

*Environmental information*

Hachette UK's policy is to use papers that are natural, renewable and recyclable products and made from wood grown in sustainable forests. The logging and manufacturing processes are expected to conform to the environmental regulations of the country of origin.

Worcester College of Technology

0149055

# Introduction

This is one of two workbooks designed to support and complement A2 courses in American government and politics. All courses cover how the USA is governed, as well as representation in the USA, and this workbook considers the second of these two.

Each of the topics contained here stands alone and may usefully be studied in any order. Consideration of the range of US elections and of voting behaviour represents the largest chapter, with many of the exercises inevitably drawing upon the 2008 elections, which were groundbreaking in so many respects. Inherent in this chapter is also evaluation of the quality of the democratic process in the USA. The next chapter covers political parties, considering the role of minor parties, but inevitably concentrating upon the internal workings, as well as the political impact, of the major parties: the Democrats and the Republicans. Pressure groups traditionally have a significant impact on the American political system, so their methods are examined in the third chapter, along with an evaluation of their implications for American democracy. Finally, how race and ethnicity impact on American politics is considered. This topic brings together many aspects from elsewhere in the course, such as the significance of the federal structure and the importance of the Supreme Court in interpreting the US Constitution, and of course, the topic has taken on an added significance since the election of President Obama.

The range of exercises can be used either during the learning process or as the basis for revision. Although the questions do not reflect the structure and style of those presented in examinations, they are designed to ensure that you have a broad knowledge and understanding of the core topics. The line allocations given to each question indicate the length of answer that is expected. Many sections also contain extension questions: the answers to these will not be found directly from the extracts provided but will either draw upon material found elsewhere in the course, or will demand some independent assessment or evaluation of material provided.

Each section ends with a 'guided essay' question. Subheadings are provided — usually with some guidance as to suitable content — to help you to plan your answer. There is, of course, never any one prescribed or 'correct' response to any particular essay question, but using the guidelines should help you to tackle questions in a systematic and coherent way. After consideration of your plan either in a group or in a one-to-one session with a tutor, you might want to write a full-length essay under examination conditions. You might then go back over the chapter and consider what other questions the examiner might ask and construct more essay plans: this is an effective method of revision. One of the features of all good essays is the use of pertinent examples to support your analysis. While we have included plenty of examples within the exercises, you should try to be aware of recent developments and how they might be relevant to your studies.

We hope that you find the material contained in this workbook both useful and stimulating, and wish you every success with your A2 exams.

# Elections and voting behaviour

## Federal elections in the USA

**1** Using the words below, complete the gaps in the text.

| | |
|---|---|
| Electoral College | 7 years |
| fixed terms | 6 years |
| 4 years | term limits (x2) |
| 14 years | 30 years |
| joint ticket | 35 years |
| mid-terms | 25 years |
| 9 years | two |
| one | 2 years (x2) |
| plurality | |

All federal elections in the USA use the first-past-the-post system, meaning that winning candidates need only a simple .................... of votes.

The president and vice-president serve ........................................ and face the electorate on the second Tuesday after the first Monday in November every ........................................ . They take office on 20 January the following year. They are elected together on a ....................................... by the nation as a whole, albeit indirectly through the ........................................ . Presidential candidates must be at least ........................................ old, must have been born in the USA and must have been resident in the USA for at least ........................................ . Since the 22nd Amendment to the Constitution, presidents are subject to ........................................ , only able to stand for election on .................... occasions.

The 435 members of the House of Representatives are subject to election every ........................................ . Elections that do not coincide with presidential elections are known as .................... . Each member represents a district within a state, with district boundaries drawn according to population. Each state is entitled to at least .................... representative. Representatives must be at least ........................................ old, have been a US citizen for at least ........................................ and be a resident of the state they represent.

There are 100 seats in the Senate, with two senators representing each of the 50 states. Senators serve for a term of ........................................ , with one-third of the Senate up for re-election every ........................................ . Senators must be at least ....................................... old, have been a US citizen for at least ........................................ and be a resident of the state they represent. Neither senators nor congressmen are subject to ........................................ .

# Electoral cycles

Because the president, the House of Representatives and the Senate are elected separately, there can often be 'divided' rather than 'unified' government; in other words, different parties control the White House and one or both of the chambers of Congress.

**Presidential and Congressional elections, 1992–2008**

| Election year | Period of office | President elected | Control of Senate | Control of House of Representatives |
|---|---|---|---|---|
| 1992 | 1993–97 | Bill Clinton (D) | Democrats | Democrats |
| 1994 | 1995–97 | | Republicans | Republicans |
| 1996 | 1997–2001 | Bill Clinton (D) | Republicans | Republicans |
| 1998 | 1999–2001 | | Republicans | Republicans |
| 2000 | 2001–05 | George W. Bush (R) | Republicans* | Republicans |
| 2002 | 2003–05 | | Republicans | Republicans |
| 2004 | 2005–09 | George W. Bush (R) | Republicans | Republicans |
| 2006 | 2007–09 | | Democrats | Democrats |
| 2008 | 2009–13 | Barack Obama (D) | Democrats | Democrats |

*Under the terms of the Constitution, the vice-president can serve as president of the Senate and thereby gain a casting vote in the event of a tie. Following the 2000 elections, both the two main parties had 50 senators and the Republicans took control of the chamber because Vice-President Dick Cheney was a Republican. In June 2001, a Republican senator (Jim Jeffords, Vermont) withdrew from the Republican Party and control of the Senate passed to the Democrats. The Republicans then regained their majority in the Senate following the mid-term elections of November 2002.

**2 a** Using the data above, identify the periods of unified government.

.....................................................................................................................................

.....................................................................................................................................

**b** Identify the periods of divided government.

.....................................................................................................................................

.....................................................................................................................................

**c** Which party controls the Senate in the event of a tie between the parties (as between January and June 2001)?

.....................................................................................................................................

.....................................................................................................................................

## Extension question

d What might be the advantages and the disadvantages of having divided government?

.............................................................................................................................................................

.............................................................................................................................................................

.............................................................................................................................................................

# Voter turnout

**Electoral turnout as a percentage of the VAP**

| Year | Turnout | Year | Turnout |
|------|---------|------|---------|
| 1960 | 63.1 | 1986 | 36.4 |
| 1962 | 47.3 | 1988 | 50.1 |
| 1964 | 61.9 | 1990 | 36.5 |
| 1966 | 48.4 | 1992 | 55.1 |
| 1968 | 60.5 | 1994 | 38.8 |
| 1970 | 46.6 | 1996 | 49.1 |
| 1972 | 55.2 | 1998 | 36.4 |
| 1974 | 38.2 | 2000 | 51.3 |
| 1976 | 53.6 | 2002 | 37.0 |
| 1978 | 37.2 | 2004 | 55.3 |
| 1980 | 52.6 | 2006 | 37.1 |
| 1982 | 39.8 | 2008 | 63.0* |
| 1984 | 53.1 | | |

Figures from *New York Times*

*Estimated figure

Figures for voter turnout in the USA are usually represented as a percentage of the voting age population (VAP), which makes them appear artificially low since most other Western countries express turnout figures as a percentage of registered voters. With a large number of illegal immigrants, as well as some states denying convicted felons the right to vote for life, the VAP in America is much larger than the number of registered voters. In addition, voters in America are responsible for their own registration.

There are also other reasons for poor turnout. Many in the poorest sections of society, as well as ethnic minorities, who have the lowest levels of turnout, are detached and alienated from the political process that they view as the preserve of the white middle classes. The first-past-the-post electoral system plus the Electoral College mean that large numbers of votes in 'safe' districts or states are effectively wasted, which may make voting in these elections appear futile. A lack of meaningful or inspiring choices may put voters off in some elections, and the large number of elections in the USA may result in 'voter fatigue'. Finally Robert Putman, in his book *Bowling Alone*, suggests that voter apathy is symptomatic of a wider process of civic decline, whereby voters have retreated into more private forms of existence.

**3 a** Describe the overall trends evident in the table, paying particular attention to the difference between presidential and mid-term elections.

...................................................................................................................................

...................................................................................................................................

...................................................................................................................................

...................................................................................................................................

**b** Why are turnout figures expressed as a percentage of the VAP likely to be lower than those expressed as a percentage of registered voters?

...................................................................................................................................

...................................................................................................................................

...................................................................................................................................

...................................................................................................................................

**c** What *five* reasons are given for relatively low turnout levels?

...................................................................................................................................

...................................................................................................................................

...................................................................................................................................

...................................................................................................................................

...................................................................................................................................

## Extension question

**d** Suggest reasons for the increase in turnout in the 2008 election.

...................................................................................................................................

...................................................................................................................................

...................................................................................................................................

...................................................................................................................................

...................................................................................................................................

# The invisible primary

In the USA, candidates for elected federal office are chosen by voters through a system of primaries and caucuses. The 'invisible primary' describes the period of positioning and campaigning that precedes an election year and the formal primary season. This period has become ever longer for presidential candidates and usually effectively starts after the previous mid-term elections. During this period, potential candidates are likely to form an exploratory committee to assess the levels of support that they would be likely to attract.

Once they have announced their candidature, they will work to secure the endorsement of key party figures and to establish name recognition more broadly through features in newspapers and magazines, as well as television appearances. They will begin to put together their campaign team, and to visit the early battlegrounds of Iowa and New Hampshire. But above all, they will begin the process of fundraising: they need to amass a 'war chest' to take them into the early primaries. It is estimated that both Barack Obama and Hillary Clinton, the two major candidates for the Democratic nomination in 2008, had each amassed a war chest in excess of $100 million before the primary season got under way.

It is widely accepted that the 'winner' of the invisible primary can be regarded as the candidate who has a fundraising advantage and a lead in the opinion polls to give him or her momentum as he or she enters the primary season. Historically, there seems to be a good correlation between the 'winner' of the invisible primary on these criteria and the eventual presidential nominee: between 1960 and 2004, there were 12 presidential elections — and hence 24 nominees from the major parties; of these 24 nominees, 20 were frontrunners before the primary season. However, recent primary elections appear to have bucked this trend. In 2004, Howard Dean took a massive fundraising advantage and a 13-point opinion-poll lead into the primaries but lost out to John Kerry. In 2008, the results were even more dramatic. Although the race was close, and Barack Obama had a phenomenal fundraising machine, all predictions before 2008 were that Hillary Clinton would win the Democratic nomination, given that her lead in the opinion polls was over 20 points throughout 2007.

The victory of John McCain in the Republican primaries was even more surprising, since he was almost forced to drop out of the race in the summer of 2007 due to lack of funds and poor polling. On the basis of the invisible primary, the Republican race should have been between Rudy Giuliani and Mitt Romney.

**4 a** When does the invisible primary take place?

.................................................................................................................................................................

.................................................................................................................................................................

**b** Identify *six* activities that candidates are likely to undertake during the invisible primary.

.................................................................................................................................................................

.................................................................................................................................................................

c How important does the invisible primary seem to be in determining the presidential candidates?

# Primaries and caucuses

Primaries and caucuses are elections held by each of the major parties in individual states to choose the party candidates for the presidential election. Each state gets a certain number of **delegates** to the parties' national conventions in the late summer, where each party's nominee is formally chosen — and the primaries and caucuses determine which candidate those delegates vote for. Some states, such as New Hampshire, have **open primaries**, in which voters can choose to vote in either the Democrat or Republican primary. Most states have **closed primaries**, in which only registered supporters of a party can vote in that party's primary. A few states, most notably Iowa, have a caucus instead of a primary. In this situation, registered party supporters gather together at various locations across the state to decide upon their preferred candidate.

The likely candidate is usually known well before all the primaries are over. In order to make their primaries 'significant', many states have been moving their primaries earlier and earlier in a process known as '**front-loading**'. In 2008, Florida and Michigan were stripped of their delegates at the Democratic Convention because they had moved their primaries forward without the permission of the Democratic National Committee. Iowa always has the first caucus — in 2008 it was on 3 January; New Hampshire has the first primary — on 8 January in 2008. Candidates who perform well in Iowa and New Hampshire often gain momentum, particularly in terms of media coverage and fundraising, which leads to success in later contests.

The Republicans award delegates on a 'winner takes all' basis: whoever wins a plurality of votes in a particular state wins all that state's delegates. However, the Democrats award delegates on a proportional basis to any candidate who wins more than 15% of the vote in a particular state. This is one of the reasons why the Democratic contest between Obama and Clinton in 2008 was so drawn out.

**5 a** Define the following terms:

delegates

......................................................................................................................................................................................

open primaries

......................................................................................................................................................................................

closed primaries

......................................................................................................................................................................................

caucus

......................................................................................................................................................................................

front-loading

......................................................................................................................................................................................

**b** Why are the Iowa caucus and the New Hampshire primary so important?

......................................................................................................................................................................................

......................................................................................................................................................................................

......................................................................................................................................................................................

**c** Why is the different way in which the two major parties award delegates significant?

......................................................................................................................................................................................

......................................................................................................................................................................................

......................................................................................................................................................................................

......................................................................................................................................................................................

# Strengths and weaknesses of the primary system

1   By allowing sections of the public to choose the candidates, primaries and caucuses strengthen democracy by increasing levels of political participation.
2   Primaries and caucuses prevent candidates from being subject to 'peer review'. State governors, senators and other senior party figures who, through their experience, can most effectively judge who could best serve as president, have been bypassed by the primary system.
3   The competing candidates in the primary elections usually offer a range of policies and strategies, and the results can give a strong indication of what appeals to the public.
4   Primary contests tend to be based on personal qualities rather than issues, therefore obscuring rather than promoting a party's message.

5   The gruelling primary contest is a good test of a candidate's energy and durability.

6   Primaries tend to test a candidate's campaigning qualities rather than his or her presidential qualities.

7   'Open' primaries give the opportunity for 'raiding' by supporters of one party voting for someone whom they perceive as a weak candidate in the other party.

8   The primaries contribute to voter fatigue and low turnout.

9   The turnout in primaries and caucuses tends to be confined to the strongest party identifiers and activists, who are unrepresentative of the general population and who tend to force candidates into more extreme policy positions.

10  The primary contests force candidates to compete across a range of different states and address political issues that are of concern to different states.

11  Since the influence of party leaders is diluted, the primaries open up the process to political 'outsiders' such as Jimmy Carter in 1976, or John McCain in 2008.

12  Too much influence is given to the voters of Iowa and New Hampshire, who are not representative of the population as a whole.

13  The process is expensive and forces candidates to raise money from vested interests.

14  Front-loading has meant that candidates must campaign in a large number of states from the beginning and has thereby increased the advantage of those with the most financial resources.

6 Decide which of the statements above could be used in support of the primary system and which might be used to criticise the system.

  a Strengths

  b Weaknesses

# The national nominating conventions

Parties usually hold a national party convention at the end of the summer during a presidential election year. It is traditional for the challenging party to hold its convention first. The conventions are attended by delegates, most of whom are chosen in primary and caucus elections and are 'pledged' to vote for a particular candidate according to the choice of the electorate in their state. There are also 'unpledged' delegates, usually senior party figures. In 2008, the Democratic primary race was so close that these unpledged 'superdelegates' were almost called upon to decide the Democratic presidential candidate.

Although the role of the conventions is formally to choose the party's presidential candidate and vice-candidate, in reality the presidential candidate is almost always already determined through primary elections, and the role of the convention is merely to confirm that nomination. The vice-presidential candidate is usually chosen by the presidential candidate rather than by the convention, although the running mate is usually announced during the convention.

The most important functions of modern conventions are the informal functions: to encourage party unity, to rally supporters prior to the official presidential campaign, and to enthuse voters. The candidate's acceptance speech is an important newsworthy event and can shape the ensuing campaign. A candidate hopes for a 'bounce' in the opinion polls following their speech.

7 Using the information from the text above, correct the following statements.

a Parties hold a national convention every year.

b The parties take it in turn to decide who holds their convention first.

c The delegates at the convention can vote for whichever candidate they like best.

d The conventions are exciting because they choose the presidential and vice-presidential candidates.

8 What four things would ideally be achieved by a candidate's acceptance speech?

# The running mate

Presidential candidates usually choose a running mate who will 'balance the ticket', i.e compensate for any individual weakness and attract voters where they perceive their own electoral appeal to be lacking. Never has this been more evident than in the 2008 presidential election. Barack Obama, the young, black, one-term senator from Illinois whom many viewed as academically elite and who had been derided by Hillary Clinton during the primaries for having insufficient understanding of foreign policy issues, chose Joe Biden, a senator for nearly 40 years and chairman of the Senate Foreign Relations Committee who was popular with the working classes. Even though he had criticised Obama during the primaries and was known for verbal gaffes, he seemed to provide the perfect balance for Obama. Senator John McCain, the Republican candidate, was mistrusted by many conservative Republicans because of his earlier liberal stances on many social issues and, if victorious, would also have been the oldest elected first-term president. He shocked the nation by declaring a relatively unknown and inexperienced governor of Alaska, Sarah Palin, as his running mate. However, as a young 'hockey mom' with impeccable conservative credentials she was a big hit with many on the right of the Republican party. The Palin nomination gave McCain a big 'bounce' in the opinion polls; the wisdom of choosing such a political novice was soon called into question, however, when Sarah Palin struggled to cope in the media spotlight. However, many observers question whether any of this really matters, since voters cast their ballot primarily on the basis of the 'top of the ticket'.

**9 a** What is meant by choosing a running mate to 'balance the ticket'?

.................................................................................................................................................................

.................................................................................................................................................................

**b** What is meant by voting according to the 'top of the ticket'?

.................................................................................................................................................................

.................................................................................................................................................................

**c** In what respects did Joe Biden 'balance the ticket' for Obama?

.................................................................................................................................................................

.................................................................................................................................................................

.................................................................................................................................................................

.................................................................................................................................................................

**d** In what respects did Sarah Palin 'balance the ticket' for McCain?

.................................................................................................................................................................

.................................................................................................................................................................

.................................................................................................................................................................

.................................................................................................................................................................

# The presidential election: the Electoral College

**10** Using the words below, complete the gaps in the text.

| | |
|---|---|
| Al Gore | majority |
| candidate | plurality |
| Congress | reapportionment |
| congressman | Senate |
| ECVs (x4) | senators |
| George W. Bush | state |
| House of Representatives | Supreme Court |
| indirect | |

The Constitution established an .................... system for electing the president. Each state is assigned Electoral College votes (ECVs) equal to their representation in both Houses of .................... . So even the smallest states such as Wyoming have a minimum of three ECVs (since they have one .................... and two ....................), whereas the largest state, California, has 55 ECVs. The number of .................... allocated to each .................... is reviewed after each 10-yearly census in a process known as ............................... . In all but two states, the winner of a .................... of votes in that state wins all the .................... of the state, even if he or she has not secured a .................... .

There are 538 .................... in total. To gain the presidency, a candidate must win more than half the total (270). The decision otherwise rests with the ......................................................, and the .................... chooses the vice-president.

The workings of the Electoral College mean that the .......................... with the most votes nationally does not necessarily win the most .................... and the presidency. This is what happened in 2000 when .................... won the popular vote but .................................... won the presidency after the .................................... controversially stopped a recount of votes in Florida.

## Assessment of the Electoral College

In the aftermath of 2000, there were renewed calls for reform of the Electoral College. Not only is it possible that the candidate with the most votes will not win the presidency, but in many years the president is elected without an overall majority of votes (for example in 1992, Clinton won with only 43% of the vote) and therefore lacks popular legitimacy. Moreover, the allocation of ECVs results in an over-representation of small states, and the winner-takes-all nature of most state-wide elections means that third-party candidates are unlikely to do well. Moreover, many voters in 'safe' states are discouraged from voting under this system.

However, the Electoral College does have the benefit of forcing candidates to gain good geographical distribution of support in order to win the election. Fundamentally, the Electoral College was established to preserve the role of individual states in choosing the president: if a direct system of 'one person one vote' were adopted for a national presidential election, then it is likely that citizens of small states would be ignored by candidates since the votes of their citizens would count for little overall. Moreover, in a direct election, the problem of a president who has not attracted a majority of the popular vote is likely to be even more pronounced, since minor candidates will feature more heavily.

**11 a** According to the text above, what are the major problems with the Electoral College?

**b** What are the strengths of the Electoral College?

## Extension question

**c** Even if the case against the Electoral College was strong, from a practical point of view, why is it unlikely to be reformed?

# Voting behaviour — long-term variables

*Voting behaviour in the 2008 presidential election*

| Group | John McCain % (R) | Barack Obama % (D) | Obama gain* |
|---|---|---|---|
| White | 55 | 43 | +2 |
| Black | 4 | 95 | +7 |
| Latino/Hispanic | 31 | 67 | +14 |
| Men | 48 | 49 | +5 |
| Women | 43 | 56 | +5 |

| Group | John McCain % (R) | Barack Obama % (D) | Obama gain* |
|---|---|---|---|
| Income under $15,000 | 25 | 73 | +10 |
| Income $15,000-$200,000 | 46 | 52 | +5 |
| Income $200,000+ | 46 | 52 | +17 |
| Age18–29 | 32 | 66 | +12 |
| Age 30–44 | 46 | 52 | +6 |
| Age 45–64 | 49 | 50 | +2 |
| Age 65+ | 53 | 45 | -2 |
| Protestant | 54 | 45 | +5 |
| Catholic | 45 | 54 | +7 |
| Jewish | 21 | 78 | +4 |
| No Religion | 23 | 75 | +8 |

Source: CNN exit polls

*Obama gain relative to vote received by Kerry in 2004

**12** Using the data in the table above, answer the following questions.

   **a** On the basis of voting behaviour in the 2008 Presidential election, which socioeconomic groups tend to disproportionately vote Republican?

   **b** Which socioeconomic groups tend to disproportionately vote Democrat?

   **c** Which were the most important groups that Obama managed to swing in his favour in order to win the presidency in 2008?

# Campaign issues

With respect to the issue that matters most in US presidential elections, Bill Clinton famously declared in 1992: 'It's the economy, stupid.' Evidence suggests that there is a lot of truth in what he said. The victory of Bill Clinton in 1992 appears to have had much to do with the poor state of the economy at the time. Likewise, his second-term victory in 1996 was in large part a vote of confidence in the state of the economy at the time. However, in 2000, the economy was successful and unemployment was low, yet Gore, the incumbent vice-president, failed to capitalise on this. And in 2004, the majority of voters reported that they preferred Kerry over Bush with respect to the economy, yet this was not enough to win the election for Kerry, since the economy had less salience — or relative importance — for the electorate at this time; more voters said that they were concerned about 'moral values' than the economy.

However, the state of the economy was certainly a salient issue in 2008 and was a significant contributory factor to Obama's success. A massive 63% cited the economy as being the major issue affecting their voting, and among these, Obama had a 9-point lead. The financial crisis that erupted in the middle of the campaign certainly helped Obama considerably: not only was McCain associated with the incumbent's perceived mishandling of the economy, but his response to the crisis portrayed him as less than calm and level-headed — in contrast with 'no drama Obama'.

Other issues that were important to the re-election of Bush in 2004 were less salient in 2008: if the issue landscape had been about foreign policy and terrorism, rather than about the economy, then McCain could have won. McCain was preferred to Obama on the issue of 'terrorism', but while 19% of voters cited this as an important factor influencing their voting in 2004, only 9% cited it as important in 2008. And while 'moral values' were the single most important issue to voters in 2004, they were low down the list of important issues in 2008, when 93% of the electorate felt that the economy was in a bad way.

**13** Explain how the state of the economy affected the following presidential elections:

   **a** 1992

   **b** 1996

   **c** 2000

   **d** 2004

   **e** 2008

**14 a** What is meant by issue 'salience'?

**b** Explain how issue salience affected the outcome of the 2008 election.

.......................................................................................................................................................

.......................................................................................................................................................

# The campaign

Presidential election campaigns are long, expensive, media-driven affairs. Although there are relatively few 'swing voters' — particularly in recent years as the main political parties and the population as a whole have become more ideologically polarised — a great deal of effort is put into attracting these voters as well as into getting out the vote of core supporters.

Election campaigns tend to concentrate on three key features:

1  **Framing the candidates**. Personality is important in American elections, and much of the campaign is focused on constructing the candidates' 'narrative' or image. In 2008, Obama's narrative was framed around his image as a self-made family man, and the themes of 'hope' and 'change'. In contrast, the Obama team framed McCain as '4 more years of Bush', out of touch and erratic. For their part, the Republicans built their candidate's narrative around his war-hero status and experience in foreign policy, as well as his 'maverick' reputation, in an attempt to distance him from the Bush years. They attempted to frame Obama as inexperienced and 'un-American' by discussing his connections with his controversial former pastor, Jeremiah Wright, for example.

2  **Targeting 'swing' states**. Many states are viewed as solidly Democrat (for example California, Massachusetts and New York), and others are solidly Republican (for example Alabama, Tennessee and South Carolina). Candidates will therefore spend the majority of their time and money campaigning in swing states such as Florida, North Carolina, Pennsylvania and Ohio. In 2008, with its vast financial advantage, as well as many more campaign offices, the Obama team was able not only to campaign heavily in the traditional swing states but also to target traditionally Republican states such as Georgia and Montana, thus diverting McCain's more limited resources from the swing states.

3  **Energising the base**. A successful campaign will inspire activists to campaign on the party's behalf, and to 'get out the vote'. Obama's 2008 campaign was particularly successful in this regard — recruiting a vast number of activists, particularly among the young, who manned telephones, raised money, knocked on doors, registered voters and then got out those voters. The selection of Biden as Obama's running mate was designed to energise the white working-class base that had hitherto been suspicious of Obama. Similarly, McCain's selection of Palin was all about mobilising the Christian Right base of the Republican party.

**15** Using the information in the text above, explain what is meant by the following terms.
   **a** framing a candidate

.......................................................................................................................................................

**b** swing states

**c** energising the base

**16** The *New York Times* (5 November 2008) described the Obama campaign as 'near flawless'. Based on the text above, what information would support this conclusion?

# The media

Some observers claim that the rise of conservative 'talk radio' shows such as those of Rush Limbaugh in the 1990s, as well as the launch and expansion of the Fox News cable television network, were some of the major factors in the growing influence of the Christian Right from the mid-1990s. Similarly, the McCain campaign repeatedly complained that the Obama campaign received favourable media coverage in 2008, and at the same time there has been a growth in popularity, and perhaps influence, of liberal television such as the satirical *Daily Show*. Moreover, the internet has seen a change in the way that voters receive their political news: there has been an explosion of political blogs, such as the liberal *Huffington Post*. However, it is difficult to say whether the media *creates* the political mood or merely monitors and reflects the political mood of the country.

One modern feature of presidential elections is the presidential and vice-presidential debates, which are broadcast live on national television. However, modern debates have become such carefully scripted, stage-managed affairs that the perceived wisdom is that they play a significant role in voting behaviour only if one of the candidates makes a notable gaffe. In the 2008 debates, both sides avoided any obvious gaffes, although McCain did appear to come close to losing his temper in the second debate, and on the whole Obama seemed to be viewed more favourably. The most eagerly awaited debate was probably the vice-presidential debate, particularly following some embarrassing television interviews that the inexperienced Sarah Palin had previously given. In fact, the expectations of Palin were so low that merely by answering the questions without making any blatant errors, her performance was deemed a success.

Probably the most notable feature of the 2008 election was not media coverage but *use* of the media by the candidates, in particular the extent to which Obama was able to massively outspend McCain, and any previous presidential candidate, in media advertising: he even ran a half-hour address on all major channels in the week of the election — costing $5 million. However, isolating the effects of media advertising from all of the other factors affecting the outcome of the election is virtually impossible. Most notable about Obama's campaign is that it will probably go down as the first true 'internet campaign' and in this respect shape all future campaigns. He created a broad grassroots movement by courting and mobilising activists, donations and voters though the internet. Democratic activists had their own dedicated Facebook page to share experiences and energise each other. Obama also used text messaging to reach voters — reminding them to vote and even announcing his choice of vice-president via a text message.

**17 a** Give *two* reasons why it is difficult to assess the impact of the media on elections.

..........................................................................................................................................................................

..........................................................................................................................................................................

..........................................................................................................................................................................

**b** Why is the impact of the presidential and vice-presidential debates on modern elections probably limited?

..........................................................................................................................................................................

..........................................................................................................................................................................

..........................................................................................................................................................................

**c** What was so revolutionary about Obama's use of the media in 2008?

..........................................................................................................................................................................

..........................................................................................................................................................................

..........................................................................................................................................................................

..........................................................................................................................................................................

# Money

Elections in the USA are massively expensive and increasingly so: the 2008 presidential election was the first $1 billion election, with Barack Obama alone raising well over half a billion dollars. There are many reasons why the elections are so expensive: the size of the country and consequent travel expenses, the duration of the campaign (including the primary phase), and the cost and growing sophistication of advertising — particularly television advertising.

Unsurprisingly, there is great concern about the growing cost of elections — not only the fear that donors may be 'buying influence', but also the fact that candidates have to expend so much time on fundraising, and the fact that many able candidates may be put off from running for office by the costs involved. Since the 1970s and the first Federal Election Campaign Act (FECA) and the establishment of the Federal Election Committee (FEC), the authorities have therefore sought to regulate fundraising, and by implication, campaign spending. The most recent legislation in this area was the Bipartisan Campaign Reform Act 2002. However, the scale of Obama's spending in 2008 might mean that the issue returns to the spotlight. The problem is that whenever the authorities try to regulate any particular source of funding, it seems to 'squeeze out' somewhere else. For example, FECA placed limits on individual contributions to campaigns, but this led to the growth of political action committees (PACs) and then to so-called '527' groups, which effectively serve to 'bundle' individual donations and then pass them to candidates. Similarly, there was an expansion of 'soft money' (non-regulated) donations for activities such as party building and get-out-the-vote (GOTV) drives, which are in reality difficult to distinguish from campaigning. 'Issue ads', which do not directly call for a vote for or against a particular candidate, but which can highlight an issue in a way that has unambiguous voting implications, also fall outside the regulations.

Candidates can receive taxpayer funding: 'matching funds' for the primary phase and total funding for the actual presidential election. However, this comes with strict limits on total spending, which is why John Kerry and George Bush both refused it in 2004, as did Barack Obama in 2008 (having previously stated that he was committed to the principle of state funding). John McCain accepted state funding and was consequently massively outspent by Obama.

**18 a** Identify *three* reasons why American elections are so expensive.

.....................................................................................................................................

.....................................................................................................................................

.....................................................................................................................................

**b** Identify *three* reasons why the growing cost of American elections might be viewed as a problem.

.....................................................................................................................................

.....................................................................................................................................

.....................................................................................................................................

**c** What general problem do the authorities face in trying to regulate election finance?

.....................................................................................................................................

.....................................................................................................................................

d Identify *three* 'loopholes' in the current legislation.

..................................................................................................................................................

..................................................................................................................................................

..................................................................................................................................................

e Why has federal funding of elections failed to 'level the playing field' as was intended?

..................................................................................................................................................

..................................................................................................................................................

## Extension question

f Can you think of what stands in the way of the federal government simply imposing state financing on candidates?

..................................................................................................................................................

..................................................................................................................................................

# Congressional elections

*Congressional elections, 1988–2008: incumbents re-elected (%)*

| Year | House of Representatives elections | Senate elections |
|------|-----------------------------------|------------------|
| 1988 | 98 | 85 |
| 1990 | 96 | 96 |
| 1992 | 88 | 83 |
| 1994 | 90 | 92 |
| 1996 | 94 | 91 |
| 1998 | 98 | 90 |
| 2000 | 98 | 79 |
| 2002 | 96 | 86 |
| 2004 | 98 | 96 |
| 2006 | 94 | 79 |
| 2008 | 95 | 93 |

Source: Centre for Responsive Politics

Many of the factors that determine voting behaviour in presidential elections will also apply in congressional elections. However, voters sometimes opt for candidates from a different party in congressional elections — perhaps even at the same election — '**splitting their ticket**'. The major feature of congressional elections is the extremely high **incumbency advantage** that is evident in the table on page 21.

There are many possible reasons for the high re-election rates of congressmen and senators. One is their ability to satisfy their constituents by '**bringing home the pork**', i.e. by using their position to secure government funding and other benefits for those living in their state or district. Incumbents also enjoy the 'franking privilege' allowing them to send six mass mailings to the constituent each year free of charge. Incumbents are likely to enjoy much greater name recognition than their competitors. They are also likely to benefit from a 'virtuous circle', whereby they attract more financial donations because they are more likely to win, but are more likely to win because they are better funded.

Finally, in many states, **gerrymandering** helps incumbents. Every decade following the census, a process of **redistricting** of congressional seats takes place, i.e. a redrawing of district boundaries according to population changes. In many states, this is the job of the state legislature, which has an incentive to redraw district boundaries to ensure more safe seats for its own party and to protect its incumbents. The manipulation of districts in this way was particularly controversial in Texas following the 2002–03 election.

**19** With reference to the text above, define the following terms:

**a** split-ticket voting

.................................................................................................................................

.................................................................................................................................

**b** incumbency advantage

.................................................................................................................................

.................................................................................................................................

**c** bringing home the pork

.................................................................................................................................

.................................................................................................................................

**d** redistricting

.................................................................................................................................

.................................................................................................................................

**e** gerrymandering

.................................................................................................................................

.................................................................................................................................

**20** According to the text on page 22, what *five* advantages do incumbents have over their competitors?

**21** Using the table on page 21, compare the re-election rates in the House and in the Senate.

## Extension question

**22** What factors might explain the difference in re-election rates identified above?

# Direct democracy in the USA

In contrast with the federal government, almost all the states employ at least some form of direct democracy. P. Fairclough, in 'Direct democracy in the USA: referendums, initiatives and recalls' (*Politics Review*, Vol. 13, No. 4), sets out the main types of direct democracy:

- **Referendums** are popular votes on measures proposed or passed by the legislature. They are commonplace in the USA, most often used when amendments are proposed to the state constitution or loans have to be raised through the issuing of bonds.
- **Initiatives**, or **propositions**, are like referendums but are proposed (initiated) by the voters themselves, usually requisite on a large number of signatures being collected. The most controversial successful propositions have been in California. Proposition 13 in 1978 cut taxes on property by almost two-thirds. In 1994, Proposition 187 denied all state services, including education and non-emergency healthcare, to illegal immigrants. In 1996, Proposition 209 ended affirmative action in all state-funded sectors. And in 2008, Proposition 8 denied the right of marriage to same-sex couples, in direct contradiction of a state Supreme Court ruling earlier that year.

- **Recall elections** allow registered voters in a state to remove an elected official from office before the end of their term, where there is evidence of corruption, negligence or, in some cases, incompetence. Although an option in several states, recall elections are rarely used, though famously in 2003 a recall election was held in California to remove Governor Gray Davis from office, to be replaced by Arnold Schwarzenegger.

**23 a** Describe in your own words the difference between a referendum and an initiative.

...........................................................................................................................................

...........................................................................................................................................

**b** Explain in your own words what a recall election is, and the circumstances under which one can be called.

...........................................................................................................................................

...........................................................................................................................................

# Evaluation of direct democracy

1 Direct democracy allows citizens to participate in the political process. This reduces popular disenchantment and alienation.
2 Political issues are often too complex and have too many varied implications to allow a simple 'yes/no' answer.
3 Decisions are more likely to be accepted if they are voted on by the people — they have greater legitimacy.
4 Referendums and initiatives force elected officials to explain fully their policy stance to those whom they represent.
5 Both recalls and initiatives can only be triggered if large numbers of signatures (usually between 5% and 15% of voters) are gathered. This type of operation can only be undertaken by well-financed lobbies and powerful commercial interests.
6 Referendums and initiatives may lead to the 'tyranny of the majority' and the suppression of minority interests.
7 Governments sometimes have to take necessary but unpopular measures. Direct democracy may preclude this.
8 Modern Western political systems — including that of the USA — are based on notions of representative democracy. Those elected to act on behalf of the people should be left to make decisions and then be judged when their period of office comes to an end.
9 In a federal system such as the USA, initiatives provide a way for legislation to reflect the differing cultures and values of different states.

**23 a** Which of the statements in the text on page 24 could be used to support direct democracy?

.................................................................................................................................................

**b** Which of the statements could be used as a criticism of direct democracy?

.................................................................................................................................................

# Guided essay

Using the subheadings and notes provided below, write an essay plan for the following question:

**The US system of elections is fair, open and democratic. Discuss.**

(Try to provide up-to-date examples to support each point of analysis.)

## Introduction

Identify the range of elections in the USA and try to establish some criteria for evaluation: what would constitute a fair, open and democratic election?

.................................................................................................................................................

.................................................................................................................................................

.................................................................................................................................................

.................................................................................................................................................

## Arguments in favour

Subject to certain qualifications, elections are open to all.

.................................................................................................................................................

.................................................................................................................................................

.................................................................................................................................................

.................................................................................................................................................

The public plays a role in selecting candidates through primaries and caucuses.

.................................................................................................................................................

.................................................................................................................................................

.................................................................................................................................................

.................................................................................................................................................

Through elections, officials are held accountable for their actions.

The system is open, and both the media and pressure groups play a role in informing the electorate.

The availability of public funding for presidential candidates opens up the system and ensures a relatively level 'playing field'.

Other points

## Arguments against

Money buys influence, and most elections are won by the best-funded candidate.

Rather than informing the electorate, the media play an undue role in influencing the electorate.

The first-past-the-post electoral system and the Electoral College mean that minor parties are unlikely to succeed.

Limitations of the Electoral College

Congressional elections favour incumbents.

Rules regarding disenfranchisement differ between states, but tend to disproportionately disenfranchise blacks.

Extent of non-registration

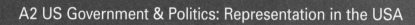

Other points

......................................................................................................................

......................................................................................................................

......................................................................................................................

......................................................................................................................

## Conclusion

Which arguments are most persuasive?

Does it vary at different elections?

What does the evidence of the most recent elections suggest?

......................................................................................................................

......................................................................................................................

......................................................................................................................

......................................................................................................................

......................................................................................................................

......................................................................................................................

......................................................................................................................

......................................................................................................................

......................................................................................................................

......................................................................................................................

......................................................................................................................

# Political parties

## The development of political parties

1 Using the words below, complete the gaps in the text.

| | |
|---|---|
| blacks | immigrants |
| business | Jews |
| campaigns | liberal (x2) |
| Catholics | New Deal coalition |
| cities | platform |
| conservatives | pragmatic |
| Constitution | re-aligned |
| Democrats | Republican |
| diverse | Republicans |
| factionalism | slavery (x2) |
| Founding Fathers | Southerners |
| government | two |
| ideological | umbrella |

Political parties were not mentioned in the ........................ . They were seen by the ................
................................ as damaging institutions that stifled debate and independent thinking and
encouraged ......................... . However, the practical reality of running election ........................
and understanding a candidate's ......................... meant that parties soon emerged. However,
the parties have ........................ on several occasions, suggesting that they are fundamentally
........................... rather than ......................... institutions.

For almost a century and a half, the USA has had ..................... major political parties: the
......................... and the ......................... . They developed into ....................... parties, each
representing a ......................... group of people. By the twentieth century, the Republicans were
the party of ......................... , resistant to change and to ......................... intervention in the
economy. Although on the whole attracting ..................... , as the party that abolished
......................... , they also had a ....................... wing. The Democrats attracted right-wing
........................... who opposed the ......................... abolition of ................... , but they also had
a ................... wing, mainly in the ................... of the North. The Democrats' .............................
............................. of the 1930s brought together these factions in addition to ......................... ,
including ................... , ......................... and ................... .

# The role of minor parties

The US political process is dominated by the two major parties. However, the USA has had over a thousand minor parties during its history, although most of them have tended to be short-lived and only a few have had a lasting impact. However, some minor parties such as the Libertarian Party and the Green Party regularly put up candidates in the vast majority of states, and even if they fail to gain federal representation, they can play a significant role in US politics in a less direct manner.

Since minor parties are able to 'think the unthinkable' in a way that the two major parties cannot, they can introduce new ideas that may capture the public imagination. For example, **Ross Perot** campaigned in the 1992 presidential election on a platform focused on balancing the federal budget. He gained no Electoral College votes in spite of attracting 19% of the popular vote. However, in light of the support he attracted, both major parties then adopted the policy of deficit reduction. In a similar fashion, **Ralph Nader** attracted only 3% of the popular vote for the Green Party in 2000, but he successfully forced the environmental issue onto the national agenda.

Moreover, just because third-party candidates are not actually elected, this does not mean that they do not have an impact on who is elected. For example, without Perot in 1992, many of his 19 million votes would probably have gone to George Bush Senior (since Perot's platform was most likely to attract disaffected Republicans), who might then have been elected instead of Clinton. Even more strikingly, in 2000, Nader polled more than 97,000 votes in Florida; it is likely that most of these would otherwise have gone to Gore and handed him the presidency.

**2 a** Identify *two* ways in which Ross Perot's candidacy in 1992 had a significant impact.

.................................................................................................................................................

.................................................................................................................................................

.................................................................................................................................................

**b** Identify *two* ways in which Ralph Nader's candidacy in 2000 had a significant impact.

.................................................................................................................................................

.................................................................................................................................................

.................................................................................................................................................

.................................................................................................................................................

## Extension question

c With reference to both Nader and Perot, assess the contention that minor parties or independents might actually have a perverse impact upon a presidential election such that their least favoured major party candidate is elected.

# The obstacles faced by minor parties

Many minor parties are characterised by factionalism and personality clashes. However, even a well-organised, unified third party would find it difficult to make a significant electoral impact.

First of all, state ballot access laws, which are designed to discourage frivolous candidates, make it difficult for minor parties to appear on all ballots. In some states, it is relatively easy to get on the ballot — in Tennessee, for example, only 25 signatures on a petition are required. However, in other states it is much harder: California requires signatures of 1% of the electorate, and New York requires signatures from every county in the state. Collecting signatures on petitions is time-consuming and costly and explains why, for example in 2000, Ralph Nader, the Green candidate, was on the ballot in only 34 states.

Even if he or she manages to get his or her name on the ballot, the first-past-the-post electoral system works against a minor-party candidate whose votes are nationally dispersed. Most notably in 1992, Perot, despite attracting 19% of the national vote, secured no Electoral College votes. Furthermore, in a race that is perceived as tight, voters are reluctant to 'waste' a vote on a minor party candidate.

No matter how dynamic their candidate, minor parties will always struggle to connect with the voters. Because the two major parties are entrenched, the media often view coverage of the minor parties as a waste of time — but without media coverage, these parties struggle to attract funding or to run a high-profile campaign. Ross Perot in 1992 is the only minor-party candidate or independent that has been allowed to participate in the televised debates. The main criterion for attracting media coverage is 'electability', but without media coverage it is difficult for minor parties to display this. Furthermore, minor parties are caught in another 'catch-22' with regard to funding: the criteria for qualifying for state funding is to have gained at least 5% of the vote in the previous election.

Finally, there is little ideological 'room' for minor parties in the USA. As broad 'umbrella' parties, most shades of moderate ideological opinion are represented within the two major parties. And since most Americans have fundamentally 'mainstream' opinions, any minor party that falls outside of this mainstream is unlikely to succeed.

3 Using your own words, explain the major barriers facing minor parties in the USA under the following headings:

a State ballot access laws

b Electoral system

c Media

d Funding

e Ideology

# Party decline or renewal?

In 1971, David Broder wrote an influential book called *The Party's Over*. He subsequently received the support of many other observers who argued that political parties in the USA had become less and less relevant. However, this sparked a backlash among other writers who argued that parties never really declined to the extent that Broder suggested, or even if they had declined, they have subsequently enjoyed a renewal.

4 Complete the table by deciding whether the statements are indicative of party decline (PD) or of party renewal (PR).

| Statement | PD/PR |
|---|---|
| a The process of nominating candidates is now undertaken by sections of the public through primaries and caucuses rather than by party leaders in 'smoke-filled rooms'. | |
| b The parties have made sustained attempts to recapture the nomination process — for example with the inclusion of 'superdelegates', nominated by senior party officials, comprising 20% of delegates at the Democratic National Convention. | |

| Statement | PD/PR |
|---|---|
| **c** Candidates' endorsement by senior party officials (for example Obama's endorsement by Senator Ted Kennedy in 2008) seems to be one of the major determinants of their performance in primary contests. | |
| **d** In the primaries, candidates establish their own campaign organisation, which they tend to continue to rely on once their nomination is secured rather than turning to their party's national committee. | |
| **e** Candidates such as George W. Bush and Barack Obama, both of whom opted out of state funding, raised most of their funds through their own organisations rather than through their parties. | |
| **f** Congressional campaigns have increasingly been centrally directed. For example, the Democrats' campaign in the 2006 mid-term elections was spearheaded by Congressman Rahm Emmanuel. | |
| **g** The Federal Election Campaign Act in 1971 weakened the financial role of parties in elections. | |
| **h** FECA amendments in 1979 allowed local and state parties to spend on 'party building' and 'get-out-the-vote' activities, which in practice are often indistinguishable from campaigning work. | |
| **i** The 2002 Bipartisan Campaign Reform Act limited the role of parties by placing limits on their ability to spend 'soft money'. | |
| **j** The role that parties have traditionally played in 'getting out the vote' has in many cases been assumed by interest groups or by activists within a candidate's personal organisation. | |
| **k** Policy development is undertaken by think tanks such as the libertarian Heritage Foundation for the Republicans or by the Economic Policy Institute for the Democrats, rather than by the parties themselves. | |
| **l** Through initiatives such as the Republicans' 'Contract with America' in 1994, and the Democrats' 'Six for '06' in 2006, the parties have established nationally agreed manifestoes for their candidates. | |

# Party identification

### Party identification, 1964–2004 (% of the population)

| | 1964 | 1976 | 1980 | 1988 | 1994 | 2000 | 2002 | 2004 |
|---|---|---|---|---|---|---|---|---|
| Strong Democrat | 27 | 15 | 18 | 17 | 15 | 19 | 17 | 17 |
| Weak Democrat | 25 | 25 | 23 | 18 | 19 | 15 | 17 | 16 |
| Independents (including those leaning towards the Democrats or Republicans) | 23 | 37 | 34 | 36 | 36 | 40 | 36 | 39 |
| Weak Republican | 14 | 14 | 14 | 14 | 15 | 12 | 16 | 12 |
| Strong Republican | 11 | 9 | 9 | 14 | 15 | 12 | 14 | 16 |

Source: National Election Studies (2004)

**5 a** Using the table on page 33, describe the trends in party identification for the period shown.

.................................................................................................................................

.................................................................................................................................

.................................................................................................................................

.................................................................................................................................

.................................................................................................................................

.................................................................................................................................

.................................................................................................................................

**b** Do the data given in the table tend to support either the party decline or the party renewal theories set out in the text on page 32?

.................................................................................................................................

.................................................................................................................................

.................................................................................................................................

.................................................................................................................................

# Parties in Congress

Parties have traditionally played a limited role in Congress. Bipartisanship was the norm in terms of getting bills passed through Congress, and party votes (where the majority of one party votes against the majority of the other party) were comparatively rare. However, in the twenty-first century Congress all of this has changed. The increased partisanship within Congress has been partly the result of a concerted effort by party organisations, in the House in particular, to more actively encourage — or even enforce — party discipline. This was notable with the Republicans in the mid-1990s under Speaker Newt Gingrich, but was taken further by speakers such as Tom 'the Hammer' DeLay, who was determined to enforce a Republican voting coalition to successfully pass the first-term legislative agenda of George W. Bush. Increased partisanship in Congress might also be a reflection of the parties themselves becoming more ideologically coherent and cohesive. It might also be a reflection of deeply controversial, polarising figures in the White House — most notably George W. Bush — as well as the predominance of deeply polarising issues within the 'culture wars' from the 1990s onwards. Nowhere was partisanship in Congress more evident than in the early days of Barack Obama's presidency. In spite of his pledge to work in a bipartisan fashion, not a single House Republican supported his key economic stimulus package — and only three Republicans Senators were brought on side to ensure the passage of the bill through the Senate.

**Party votes in Congress as a percentage of total, selected years**

| Year | House | Senate |
|------|-------|--------|
| 1970 | 27 | 35 |
| 1976 | 36 | 37 |
| 1979 | 47 | 47 |
| 1990 | 49 | 54 |
| 1994 | 62 | 52 |
| 2000 | 43 | 49 |
| 2006 | 55 | 56 |
| 2007 | 62 | 60 |
| 2008 | 53 | 52 |

**6 a** From the table above, describe the general trend in the proportion of party votes in the House and Senate.

..............................................................................................................................................

..............................................................................................................................................

..............................................................................................................................................

**b** Does the trend in party voting in Congress support either the party decline or the party renewal thesis set out in the 'Party decline or renewal?' text on page 32?

..............................................................................................................................................

**c** Why has there been increased polarisation in Congress?

..............................................................................................................................................

..............................................................................................................................................

..............................................................................................................................................

..............................................................................................................................................

# Party factions and ideologies

The major political parties have become more ideologically cohesive and more ideologically distinct from each other in recent years, with the Republican Party becoming recognisable as conservative and the Democrats as more liberal. However, there remain distinct factions within the parties.

The Republican Party is dominated by two strands: social conservatives believe that everyone needs clear moral guidance, strong effective leadership and disincentives to give in to selfish desires; fiscal conservatives argue that excessive government intervention undermines incentives and creates a culture of dependency resulting in economic decline. Outside of these groups, neo-conservatives focus on the importance of foreign policy and feel that the USA has a responsibility to challenge regimes hostile to its interests and values. There are also 'nativist' factions within the Republican Party, whose main focus is to strongly oppose large-scale immigration.

Members of the Democratic Party are traditionally more willing to promote change and innovation alongside greater positive government action to provide welfare and to regulate business. However Blue Dog Democrats, on the right wing of the party, appear to have more in common with Republicans on many issues: they tend to be pro-gun and anti-abortion and were key to taking seats in former Republican strongholds in the 2006 mid-terms. The Democratic Leadership Council, often associated with the Clintons, is much more liberal on social issues than the Blue Dogs. To the left of the DLC are the Liberal Democrats, who advocate free trade, a less militaristic foreign policy and more forceful promotion of civil liberties. Barack Obama is a Progressive Democrat: opposing the Iraq war, opposing corporate influence in government and supporting universal healthcare and greater social and economic equality generally. On the far left of the Democratic party is the 'Internet Left' — a grassroots movement that believes that the Democrats should actively fight against conservative policies, especially on moral issues.

**7 a** Identify *four* factions within the Republican Party and what they stand for.

...................................................................................................................................................

...................................................................................................................................................

...................................................................................................................................................

...................................................................................................................................................

...................................................................................................................................................

...................................................................................................................................................

**b** Identify *five* factions within the Democratic Party and what they stand for.

...................................................................................................................................................

...................................................................................................................................................

...................................................................................................................................................

...................................................................................................................................................

...................................................................................................................................................

...................................................................................................................................................

...................................................................................................................................................

**8** Complete the table by deciding whether mainstream Democrats (D) or Republicans (R) are likely to support the policies listed.

| Policy | D/R |
|---|---|
| **a** Affirmative action | |
| **b** Tax rises in order to increase spending on education | |
| **c** Restrictions on the availability of abortion | |
| **d** Unilateralism — where the USA takes action across the world without first securing the agreement of traditional allies | |
| **e** Healthcare reform for all, based on greater government provision | |
| **f** An amendment to the US Constitution prohibiting same-sex marriage | |
| **g** School vouchers allowing more parental choice in education and encouraging competition between schools | |
| **h** A large increase in federal government spending in order to pull the US economy out of recession | |

# Guided essay

Using the subheadings and notes provided below, write an essay plan for the following question:

**To what extent has there been a resurgence of political parties in the USA?**

(Try to provide up-to-date examples to support each point of analysis.)

## Introduction

Historical background: parties are not mentioned in the Constitution and developed as loose coalitions.

## Context: party decline

The idea of 'resurgence' makes no sense unless parties were at some point weak. In this context, outline the main tenets of Broder's 'party decline' thesis.

....................................................................................................

....................................................................................................

....................................................................................................

## Ways in which parties may be seen as stronger

(Try to *qualify/evaluate* each point as it is made.)

Development of centralised organisations, RNC and DNC:
- in candidate selection process

....................................................................................................

....................................................................................................

....................................................................................................

- in campaign process

....................................................................................................

....................................................................................................

....................................................................................................

- in development of 'manifestoes'

....................................................................................................

....................................................................................................

....................................................................................................

Party unity in Congress, and hence greater role for parties in legislative process

....................................................................................................

....................................................................................................

....................................................................................................

....................................................................................................

....................................................................................................

Ideological polarisation of parties, and perhaps of the nation

Other factors

## Conclusion

Address the 'resurgence' issue: was the party ever 'over' in the first place? Are the arguments that parties are now stronger convincing? Does it all depend upon the personalities/political circumstances of the time?

# Pressure groups

## Categorising pressure groups

US pressure groups (or interest groups, as they are often called) are usually categorised according to their membership and their aims. **Institutional pressure groups** seek to protect the interests of their own members. They include business groups, labour unions, including the umbrella organisation AFL–CIO (American Federation of Labor–Congress of Industrial Organizations), and groups representing the various professions. In contrast, **membership** or **promotional groups** either seek to promote the perceived interests of others or have broader ideological aims. They include **think tanks** that conduct research, write articles, publish journals and organise conferences — usually with a particular ideological slant — in an attempt to influence those with political power. For example, the Heritage Foundation and the American Enterprise Institute are important conservative think tanks, whereas the Brookings Institute and the Institute for Policy Studies are more liberal.

1 Using the information in the text above, place each of the following interest groups in the appropriate category in the table below.

| | |
|---|---|
| National Rifle Association (NRA) | National Association for the Advancement of Colored People (NAACP) |
| National Association of Manufacturers (NAM) | American Bar Association (ABA) |
| American Association of Retired Persons (AARP) | Mothers Against Drink Driving (MADD) |
| US Chamber of Commerce | American Civil Liberties Union (ACLU) |
| National Farmers' Union (NFU) | Christian Voice |
| American Medical Association (AMA) | United Auto Workers (UAW) |

*Categorising interest groups*

| Institutional groups | | Membership groups | |
|---|---|---|---|
| **Type** | **Examples** | **Type** | **Examples** |
| Business groups | | Single-issue groups | |
| Labor unions | | Ideological groups | |
| Professional groups | | Group rights groups | |

# The importance of pressure groups in the USA

*Congress shall make no law respecting an establishment of religion, or prohibiting the free exercise thereof; or abridging the freedom of speech, or of the press; or the right of the people peacefully to assemble and to petition the government for redress of grievances.*
Amendment 1 of the US Constitution

Perhaps the fact that the right to assemble and to petition the government for redress of grievances is enshrined in the First Amendment is one of the reasons why there is estimated to be in excess of 100,000 interest groups in the USA, and why the vast majority of Americans belong to more than one. Not only is the political culture of the USA firmly rooted in the ideas of liberty, democracy and civic responsibility, but the diversity of American society in terms of ethnicity, religion and socioeconomic background means that interest groups have emerged to reflect this diversity.

Moreover, the American political system provides particular opportunities for pressure group influence. The fragmented structure of American government provides numerous points of access for interest groups at federal, state and local level. They might also have access to the judicial branch: by directly sponsoring cases, by providing *amicus curiae* (friends of the court) briefs in order to try to influence rulings, or even by attempting to influence judicial appointments. In many states, interest groups can also sponsor initiatives as part of the democratic process.

Many Americans might feel they have grievances that they need to express through pressure group activity. This might be the case because a traditionally weak party system has often failed to adequately fulfil the representative needs of the people. Moreover, the number of 'wasted votes' within the electoral system might make many citizens feel effectively disenfranchised; membership of pressure groups might be viewed as a way of trying to redress this balance. Finally, the rapid expansion in the scale and scope of government activity since the 1930s has meant that more people feel the impact of government activity in their everyday lives, and that expectations of government have increased.

2 Using the information in the text above, identify *twelve* reasons why there is so much pressure group activity in the USA.

..................................................................................

..................................................................................

..................................................................................

..................................................................................

# Interest group methods

## Public campaigns

Public campaigns are used to stir up public opinion and to put legislators under pressure. Most famously, the **March on Washington** in 1963 was an integral part of the civil rights movement. This was replicated by the **Million Mom March** on Washington in favour of gun control in 2000. However, public demonstrations might be counterproductive, especially where they frighten people (such as some of the more extreme strategies used by the anti-abortion group **Operation Rescue**), or where they are indicative that other, more direct access to decision makers is not open to them.

Public campaigns might be carried out in other ways — for example, groups such as the NRA make extensive use of television advertising. Right-to-life groups used sophisticated computerised mailing systems to target sympathisers in a high-profile campaign to save the life of **Terri Schiavo** in 2005. In 24 states, interest groups have the opportunity to directly change the law through initiatives or propositions. For example, in 2008 a coalition of conservative pressure groups such as the **Family Research Council** successfully campaigned to pass Proposition 8, which outlawed same-sex marriage in California.

**3 a** Identify *four* different activities that might come under the heading 'public campaigns'.

..................................................................................

..................................................................................

..................................................................................

..................................................................................

**b** Why might street protests be a sign of weakness rather than strength?

..................................................................................

..................................................................................

## Lobbying

A lobbyist is a paid organisation or individual that attempts to influence legislators or members of the executive branch on behalf of individuals and pressure groups, in particular by establishing and exploiting long-term relationships with key decision makers. The lobbying industry is vast — centred on 'K Street' in Washington — and the size and scale of lobbying activities has led to fears that both the legislative and executive branches of government are effectively controlled by the lobbyists. The lobbying industry is therefore subject to extensive regulation — in particular requiring the registration of lobbyists and the disclosure of activities. However, the high-profile conviction for fraud of top lobbyist **Jack Abromoff** in 2006 led to calls for a further tightening of regulation. There is particular concern about the so-called '**revolving door**' phenomenon, whereby members of the legislature and the executive leave their posts in order to use their contacts to take up lucrative contracts with lobbyists.

**4 a** What is a lobbyist?

..............................................................................................................................................................

..............................................................................................................................................................

**b** Why is it seen as necessary to regulate the lobbying industry?

..............................................................................................................................................................

..............................................................................................................................................................

**c** What is meant by the 'revolving door' phenomenon?

..............................................................................................................................................................

..............................................................................................................................................................

## Extension question

**d** Why do you think that it has proven so difficult to regulate and to restrict the growth of the lobbying industry in the USA?

..............................................................................................................................................................

..............................................................................................................................................................

..............................................................................................................................................................

## The courts

Both the nature of the American political system and the generally litigious character of US society make using the courts a popular method for interest groups. For example, they might seek a ruling that an action is unconstitutional; in *Reno* v *American Civil Liberties Union* (1997), the Supreme Court struck down two provisions of the 1996 Communications and Decency Act on the basis that they violated the First Amendment. Interest groups might also **sponsor cases** brought by third parties: most notably the NAACP sponsored the *Brown* v *Board of Education* case, which ruled against segregation in schools in 1954. *Amicus curiae* (friends of the court) briefs can be submitted by a pressure group in order to highlight a particular issue that might influence a ruling. For instance, 350 *amicus curiae* briefs representing the views of pressure groups, including one representing the Fortune 500 companies, were filed in the *Grutter* v *Bollinger* affirmative action ruling in 2003. Finally, interest groups might attempt to influence the appointment of federal judges. For example, urged on by liberal pressure groups such as People for the American Way, Democratic senators blocked (through filibuster) ten of Bush's federal court nominations between 2002 and 2005.

**5** Identify ways in which the following pressure groups have achieved influence through the judicial branch:

  **a** The ACLU

  ....................................................................................................................................

  ....................................................................................................................................

  **b** The NAACP

  ....................................................................................................................................

  ....................................................................................................................................

  **c** Fortune 500 companies

  ....................................................................................................................................

  ....................................................................................................................................

  **d** People for the American Way

  ....................................................................................................................................

  ....................................................................................................................................

## Influencing elections

Many interest groups are heavily involved in election campaigns through **financial contributions** to candidates. For example Emily's List (which campaigns to enhance female representation in Congress) gave $11 million to the Democrats in 2008, whereas American Solutions to Winning the Future, a conservative group, gave $20 million to the Republicans. Legislation restricting the amount that individuals can give directly to candidates has led to the growth of **Political Action Committees** as well as **527** groups (named after a clause in the tax code), which serve to gather together donations and spend them in a way that garners sympathy for the interests of the PAC and 527 contributors. For example, there is a Friends of the Earth PAC and a Laborers Union PAC. Emily's List is a 527 group, as was MoveOn.Org, an influential anti-Bush group.

Interest groups might also work to **shape the agenda** of a particular election. For example, the Christian Right successfully focused the 2004 presidential election campaign on moral issues. The same groups were highly successful in their **voter mobilisation** drives in 2004. Pressure groups may also campaign to **influence a candidate's image**; for example the 'Swift Boat Veterans' were so successful in destroying John Kerry's war hero image in 2004 that 'to swift boat' a candidate has almost become a verb in US election campaigns.

**6 a** Explain what PACs and 527 groups are.

.................................................................................................................................

.................................................................................................................................

.................................................................................................................................

**b** Identify *four* ways in which interest groups might attempt to influence the outcome of elections.

.................................................................................................................................

.................................................................................................................................

.................................................................................................................................

.................................................................................................................................

# Interest groups and the 2008 election

In contrast to previous elections, interest groups do not appear to have had a significant impact on the outcome of the 2008 presidential election. This is mainly because Obama's highly effective fundraising machine largely eclipsed the need for funding from pressure groups. Moreover, the Bipartisan Campaign Reform Act 2002 had further restricted 'soft money' donations to political parties. Most 527 money that was raised was channelled to the Democrats: it is possible that many conservative groups were reluctant to give money to a campaign finance reformer (John McCain) who, through his BCRA, had effectively tried to regulate them out of business.

Interest group efforts to shape the agenda of the election had little success in 2008, simply because the economic crisis eclipsed all other issues. The gravity of the economic downturn meant that there was no room for 'post-material' issues such as moral values or even Iraq. In addition, it was the candidates themselves that shaped their own — and their opponents' — image in 2008. The most memorable television advertisements — such as Obama's 'infomercial', McCain's 'celebrity ad' and even Clinton's '3 a.m. ad' — came from the candidates themselves rather than from pressure groups.

Interest groups typically play an 'attack dog' role in presidential elections. However, the Obama campaign had the money and the organisation to respond to the various interest group attacks, such as the so-called 'Muslim attack'. Moreover, interest group attacks on Obama lacked impact since they did not share a similar theme: some dealt with his position on Iraq, some with his associations (such as his former pastor Jeremiah Wright) and yet others with his domestic issue positions.

Finally, in 2008, both parties, and their candidates, had large get-out-the-vote operations of their own: they did not need interest groups to mobilise voters. It is perhaps for all of the reasons discussed that many interest groups chose to focus their energies on Congressional elections in 2008.

**7 a** What is meant by the statement 'interest groups typically play an "attack dog" role in presidential elections'?

..................................................................................................................................................

..................................................................................................................................................

**b** Identify *eight* reasons why interest groups failed to have a significant impact on the 2008 presidential election.

..................................................................................................................................................

..................................................................................................................................................

..................................................................................................................................................

..................................................................................................................................................

..................................................................................................................................................

..................................................................................................................................................

..................................................................................................................................................

..................................................................................................................................................

## Extension question

**c** Suggest reasons why interest groups might play a more significant role in future presidential election campaigns.

..................................................................................................................................................

..................................................................................................................................................

..................................................................................................................................................

..................................................................................................................................................

..................................................................................................................................................

# Why are some pressure groups more influential than others?

It is difficult to assess or to compare the 'influence' or 'success' of pressure groups, let alone to identify which factors contribute to such success. The size of a pressure group's membership, and hence the numbers that it purports to represent, can be important. For example, AARP is widely regarded as highly influential because it has a membership of over 35 million people and can therefore legitimately claim to speak on behalf of America's pensioners. In contrast, it is widely accepted that the influence of America's labour unions has waned as their membership has declined in recent years. However, AIPAC (American

Israel Public Affairs Committee) has a modest 100,000 members yet is disproportionately influential in aspects of US foreign policy, while the NRA's longstanding influence stems not so much from the number of members (less than 4 million) but from the fact that they have an exceptionally well-motivated and well-organised grassroots network.

The influence of a pressure group will also depend on the extent to which it has public support — and even on where that support is concentrated. For example, environmental groups have enjoyed much more success in California than in many other states, simply because they have more public support there, while AARP is influential partly because its supporters are concentrated within several districts of the swing state of Florida.

A particular pressure group's influence is also likely to vary according to the administration: thus pressure groups associated with the Christian Right, which were highly influential under Bush, are unlikely to wield the same kind of influence within the Obama administration.

America's political system means that pressure groups are always more likely to be successful in blocking unfavourable legislation than in promoting desired legislation. Nowhere is this more notable than with respect to healthcare, where groups representing the insurance industry, the pharmaceutical industry and medical professionals have repeatedly blocked reform.

But the most important factor giving 'clout' to pressure groups is their financial resources. AARP, AIPAC and the NRA all partly owe their influence to spending power. Not only can money be directed towards campaign contributions in elections, but it can also purchase the services of professional lobbyists to gain access to Washington's decision makers.

**8 a** Why is it difficult to assess the success of individual pressure groups?

.......................................................................................................

.......................................................................................................

.......................................................................................................

.......................................................................................................

**b** Suggest *three* reasons why membership numbers are not necessarily a reliable indicator of pressure group influence.

.......................................................................................................

.......................................................................................................

.......................................................................................................

.......................................................................................................

.......................................................................................................

.......................................................................................................

c Identify *three* reasons why AARP is particularly influential.

.................................................................................................................................................

.................................................................................................................................................

.................................................................................................................................................

d Give *two* reasons why financial resources might be important to a pressure group's success.

.................................................................................................................................................

.................................................................................................................................................

## Extension question

e What features of America's political system make it easier for a pressure group to block legislation than to achieve new legislation?

.................................................................................................................................................

.................................................................................................................................................

.................................................................................................................................................

.................................................................................................................................................

# Pressure groups and the democratic process

From one perspective, the USA may be viewed as the ultimate **pluralist society**: a large number of pressure groups strengthen representation, have competitive access to decision makers and are a dynamic force for change. Nevertheless, there are many critics of the role that pressure groups play in the US political system. This criticism takes two general forms: criticism from the left — the **elitist perspective** — suggests that some groups (particularly corporate magnates and financial capital) are systematically favoured over others; while criticism from the right suggests that interest groups have served to **distort market forces** and have forced excessively 'big government'. A third criticism suggests that competing pressure groups have resulted in **demosclerosis** or **hyperpluralism** — whereby the number of competing interest groups is effectively 'choking' government and preventing much-needed reform — since every government action is subject to scrutiny and criticism by some pressure group.

### The impact of pressure groups
1   Interest groups serve to increase political participation.
2   Influence is limited to those groups with large memberships, effective lobbyists, effective lawyers and considerable wealth.

3 The 2001 Energy Task Force, headed by Dick Cheney, was dominated by commercial interests — only one meeting was held with environmental organisations, as opposed to over 40 meetings with large oil companies.

4 Pressure group activity ensures that national and state governments stay in touch with public opinion, as well as providing a valuable source of expertise.

5 Interest groups ensure that minority views are heard and hence prevent 'tyranny of the majority'.

6 Through their unions, public-school teachers have been able to dictate their own terms and conditions and restrict the introduction of school voucher schemes that would serve to promote competition and drive up standards.

7 It has become virtually impossible to get good-quality, independent advice, since everyone is linked to a pressure group — this has therefore led to poorer government.

8 Pressure groups have managed to secure tax advantages and government subsidies for their members at the cost of the nation's economic performance and other taxpayers.

9 Entrenched interests have led to stalemate and political stagnation: this can clearly be seen with the failure of Hillary Clinton's healthcare reforms and of George W. Bush's immigration and welfare reforms.

10 Interest groups prevent stagnation and propose innovative policies: civil rights legislation would never have happened without the activities of groups such as the NAACP.

11 Technological developments such as the internet make interest group politics more accessible than ever before.

12 Interest group contributions to elections enhance the idea that politicians are for sale and increase the cynicism about the political system in general.

**9** From the list above, identify which of the arguments would be used to support:

a the pluralist perspective in defence of pressure groups

.................................................................................................................................

b the elitist perspective criticising pressure groups

.................................................................................................................................

c the right-wing perspective criticising pressure groups for their distortion of market forces

.................................................................................................................................

d the demosclerosis perspective that pressure groups restrict all government activity

.................................................................................................................................

# Guided essay

Using the subheadings and notes provided below, write an essay plan for the following question:

**How influential a role do pressure groups play in contemporary American politics?**

(Try to provide up-to-date examples to support each point of analysis.)

## Introduction
Give some indication of the number and range of interest groups in the USA, and try to identify some criteria for evaluation by establishing what is meant by 'influential' — for example determining public opinion/the outcome of elections/policy/legislation. You might also mention difficulties involved in establishing 'influence'.

..........................................................................................................................

..........................................................................................................................

..........................................................................................................................

## Arguments that pressure groups play an influential role
Through campaign contributions, by their own advertising to set the agenda, and by GOTV drives, interest groups can influence the outcome of elections.

..........................................................................................................................

..........................................................................................................................

..........................................................................................................................

The US political system offers many points of access and hence many opportunities for pressure group influence, for example at national, state and local level; access to the executive, the legislature and the judiciary.

..........................................................................................................................

..........................................................................................................................

..........................................................................................................................

Interest groups can drive the agenda of an administration (for example the Christian Right and the George W. Bush administration).

..........................................................................................................................

..........................................................................................................................

..........................................................................................................................

Group activity has *led to* some important social and political reforms (lots of examples).

.................................................................................................

.................................................................................................

.................................................................................................

.................................................................................................

Interest group activity has been influential by *preventing* social reform, for example healthcare reform.

.................................................................................................

.................................................................................................

.................................................................................................

.................................................................................................

Other points

.................................................................................................

.................................................................................................

.................................................................................................

.................................................................................................

## Arguments that pressure groups do not play an influential role

The role that interest groups play in elections is often exaggerated (e.g. 2008 election).

.................................................................................................

.................................................................................................

.................................................................................................

.................................................................................................

Since many interest groups have a countervailing interest group (for example pro-choice and anti-abortion groups), their activities effectively cancel each other out.

.................................................................................................

.................................................................................................

.................................................................................................

.................................................................................................

Much government activity happens in spite of rather than because of pressure group activity (for example the Iraq war).

Regulation — for example of campaign finance and lobbying activities, as well as 'open government' legislation — has effectively curbed the influence of pressure groups.

Other points

## Conclusion

Include some weighting of various arguments. Also note that it is likely that some groups are more influential than others, that this will probably vary over different time periods and with different administrations, and that a conclusion that pressure groups *are* influential could be viewed either positively or negatively.

# Racial and ethnic politics

## The USA — a diverse society

In a celebrated comment, President John F. Kennedy described the USA as a 'nation of immigrants'. While the early colonies were largely British in character, the American nation has been repeatedly reshaped and restructured by successive waves of newcomers.

Over the past few decades, immigrants arriving in the USA have been disproportionately drawn from the Spanish-speaking countries of Central and South America. Some observers, such as Samuel Huntington, author of the 2004 book *Who Are We? The Challenges to America's National Identity*, suggest that this has significant cultural and political implications for the character of the USA. Whereas early immigrants could only advance and prosper if they worked hard, learned English and were assimilated, today's Latino immigrants, it is said, have maintained close cultural ties with their former country and remain largely unassimilated.

African Americans differ from most other racial groups in the USA since, for the most part, they were not immigrants but instead arrived in captivity as slaves during the seventeenth, eighteenth and nineteenth centuries, and the southern economy — which was largely agricultural — came to depend on slave labour.

### US population by race and ethnicity (%)

| Racial/ethnic group | 1980 | 1990 | 2000 | 2050 (estimated) |
|---|---|---|---|---|
| White (non-Hispanic) | 79.6 | 75.7 | 69.1 | 50.1 |
| Black | 11.5 | 11.8 | 12.2 | 14.6 |
| Hispanic/Latino | 6.4 | 9.0 | 12.6 | 24.4 |
| Asian | 1.5 | 2.8 | 3.8 | 8.0 |

Source: US Census Bureau (2000, 2003)

NB: *figures do not add up to 100% because some people do not fall into any of these categories, and others belong to more than one category.*

1 a How did President John F. Kennedy describe the USA?

.................................................................................................................................

b In what way do critics of US policy suggest that the immigrants of today differ from those who arrived in the USA during the nineteenth century?

.................................................................................................................................

.................................................................................................................................

c Why are most African Americans not described as 'immigrants'?

.................................................................................................................................

d How has the racial/ethnic composition of the USA changed in recent years?

..................................................................................................................................

..................................................................................................................................

..................................................................................................................................

e How is the racial/ethnic composition of the USA expected to change up to 2050?

..................................................................................................................................

..................................................................................................................................

..................................................................................................................................

## Extension question

f Why is the racial composition of the USA becoming increasingly difficult to measure?

..................................................................................................................................

..................................................................................................................................

# The history of African Americans in the USA

2 Using the words below, complete the gaps in the text.

| | |
|---|---|
| Abraham Lincoln | Jim Crow laws |
| *Brown v Board of Education of Topeka* | Little Rock High School, Arkansas |
| Civil Rights Act | Lyndon Johnson |
| Civil Rights Amendments | March on Washington |
| civil rights movement | Martin Luther King |
| Civil War | Montgomery |
| Constitutional Convention | NAACP |
| *Dred Scott v Sandford* | *Plessy v Ferguson* (x2) |
| Jamestown | Voting Rights Act |

........................... , the first British colony, introduced slavery to the USA. Pilgrims in the north of the country were against slavery. No agreement on slavery could be reached at the

...................................................... , 1787, hence the compromise agreed to was to leave the issue to the states' discretion. The Supreme Court ruled in ........................................... ,1857, that slaves were not entitled to their freedom, even if they left their home state. The election of

......................................... as president in 1860 brought the issue of slavery to a head and led to the secession of the South and the outbreak of the ............................... .

Following the victory of the Union states, slavery was formally abolished in 1863. The ..................................................... of 1865, 1868 and 1870 incorporated the ban on slavery into the Constitution, guaranteed full rights to all citizens and gave blacks the right to vote. However, following the withdrawal of Union troops from the South in 1877, *de jure* or legal segregation was established. Segregation existed in schools, hospitals, libraries, transport, restaurants, hotels and swimming pools. The .......................................... ruling, 1896, allowed for 'separate but equal' facilities, in effect allowing segregation to continue. ....................................... effectively disenfranchised blacks.

The .................... was established in 1909, to build a 'beloved society' and to end *de facto* segregation (segregation in practice) as well as *de jure* segregation. The ....................................... ............................... ruling in 1954 effectively overturned the earlier ......................................... ruling, but required federal troops to enforce it. This triggered the ............................................. of 1954 to 1968, which used peaceful protest to highlight the issues of segregation. Key moments in the civil rights movement were the ......................... bus boycott, lunch counter sit-ins, enrolment of seven black students at ................................................................. , and the ............................................... culminating in .........................................'s famous speech. ........................................ signed the ................................... 1964 and the ......................................... 1965, which formally ended *de jure* segregation and discrimination.

# Affirmative action

You do not wipe away the scars of centuries by saying: now you are free to go where you want, do as you desire, choose the leaders you please. You do not take a person who, for years, has been hobbled by chains and liberate him, bring him to the starting line and then say: 'you are free to compete with the others', and still justly believe that you have been completely fair. Thus it is not enough just to open the gates of opportunity. All our citizens must have the ability to walk through those gates. This is the next and more profound stage of the battle for civil rights. We seek not just freedom but opportunity — not just equality as a right and a theory but equality as a fact and a result.

President Lyndon B. Johnson, 1965

Although the Voting Rights Act 1965 effectively marked the end of *de jure* discrimination, the **Kerner Report 1968** found evidence of significant *de facto* discrimination remaining. The report urged the federal government to tackle the disadvantages faced by blacks — particularly in the areas of housing, employment opportunities, education, poverty, family breakdown, crime and drug use.

**Johnson's Great Society** programme was an attack on poverty. Schemes like Medicare, Medicaid and the Employment Opportunity Act benefitted blacks in particular. The Housing and Urban Development Act 1968, and the Fair Housing Act 1968 provided more public housing and outlawed discrimination in the sale and rental of housing.

**President Nixon** went further, from 1969 effectively ushering in a period of **affirmative action**: the idea that not only should previously disadvantaged ethnic groups have equal opportunities to other groups and equal access to public services but that their opportunities should be enhanced in order to counteract their previous disadvantage. The first step along the road of affirmative action came with Nixon's **Philadelphia Plan** in 1969, which required contractors doing business with the federal government to have 'goals and timetables' for the hiring of minorities. Affirmative action was approved by the Supreme Court in several rulings — the landmark ruling being *Swann v Charlotte-Mecklenburg Board of Education* **(1971)**, which allowed 'busing' (transporting students to schools other than their local high school in order to provide a better racial mix) to end *de facto* segregation in schools.

**3 a** Summarise President Johnson's argument in his 1965 speech.

.................................................................................................................

.................................................................................................................

.................................................................................................................

**b** What is meant by affirmative action?

.................................................................................................................

.................................................................................................................

.................................................................................................................

**c** What is significant about the *Swann v Charlotte-Mecklenburg* Supreme Court ruling?

.................................................................................................................

.................................................................................................................

.................................................................................................................

## Extension question

**d** How do you think (a) liberals, (b) conservatives view affirmative action?

.................................................................................................................

.................................................................................................................

.................................................................................................................

.................................................................................................................

# The shift away from affirmative action

The shift of power back towards the states from the time of Nixon onwards (under his policy of 'New Federalism') saw power move towards elected representatives who were less inclined (in the South in particular) to do much for the cause of civil rights. In addition, under Reagan from 1980, federal government was less convinced of the merits of affirmative action. Moreover, the Supreme Court became less inclined to support affirmative action in its rulings — particularly the Rehnquist Court from 1986. Finally, the people themselves appeared to turn against affirmative action, with many state initiatives from the late 1990s onwards banning affirmative action in state-supported programmes (for example Michigan in 2006).

The key legal turning point came with the *University of California v Bakke* (1978) ruling, which declared that although racial considerations were a legitimate factor in university admissions, the use of rigid quotas was not acceptable. This outlawing of so-called 'mechanistic' affirmative action programmes was reinforced by two rulings in 2003: *Gratz v Bollinger* and *Grutter v Bollinger*, which ruled that admissions to the University of Michigan were unconstitutional because they automatically awarded 20 of the 150 points needed for admission to students from minority backgrounds; however, race was still allowed to be considered as a factor on an 'individualistic' basis.

It has not only been affirmative action in education admission policies that has proven controversial. In *City of Richmond v J. A. Croson Co.* (1989), Richmond City Council's policy of ensuring that 30% of contracts went to minority-owned firms was overturned and this ruling was applied to the federal government in *Adarand Constructors v Pena* (1995). Most recently in the case *Parents involved in Community Schools v Seattle School District No. 1 et al.* (2007) the Supreme Court narrowly ruled (5–4) that the race of a child cannot be used to determine where he or she is sent to school. This effectively overturned the Swann ruling — and according to some the *Brown v Board* ruling — but the narrowness of the decision shows how divided the Supreme Court, and indeed society as a whole, remains over the issue of affirmative action.

**4 a** Identify *four* reasons why there has been a shift away from affirmative action programmes in recent years.

...............................................................................................................................................

...............................................................................................................................................

...............................................................................................................................................

**b** What was so significant about the *Bakke*, *Gratz* and *Grutter* rulings?

...............................................................................................................................................

...............................................................................................................................................

...............................................................................................................................................

c What was so significant about the *Seattle Schools* ruling?

.................................................................................................................................................

.................................................................................................................................................

.................................................................................................................................................

# Debating affirmative action

There are essentially three views regarding the appropriateness of affirmative action policies:
a   Affirmative action is still necessary.
b   Affirmative action was appropriate when first introduced but has now run its course.
c   Affirmative action does not work, is inherently unfair and damages whites, blacks and society in general.
Democrats tend to split themselves between strands **a** and **b**, whereas Republicans tend to be against all forms of affirmative action.

**5 a** Decide which strand of opinion is best represented by the following statements and complete the table accordingly.

| Statements concerning the merits of affirmative action (AA) | a/b/c |
|---|---|
| Continuing inequality is evidence of the failure of AA. | |
| Continuing inequality is evidence that AA needs to go further. | |
| AA breeds resentment among all races. | |
| AA has compensated for the injustices of the past and there is now equality of opportunity in the USA, even if there is not equality of outcome. | |
| AA encourages laziness among many African Americans and undermines the achievements of those African Americans that are successful. | |
| AA means that university places and jobs are not always filled by the most deserving and most talented. | |
| AA was designed to focus on the African American community, but poverty and disadvantage are now spread across all ethnic and racial groups. | |
| Any form of discrimination, including 'reverse discrimination', is inherently unjust and morally wrong. | |
| Blacks remain under-represented in senior positions — for example, there is now no elected black senator. | |
| The Constitution protects equality of opportunity. | |
| While it was systematically abused in the past, that is no longer true of the African American community, which now needs to look inside itself to understand its continuing social and economic problems. | |
| AA promotes a culture of dependence. | |
| The black community is now hugely represented in sport, film, music and even politics. If any ethnic group is under-represented in US society, it is the Hispanics. | |

## Extension question

**b** What does the election of President Barack Obama suggest about the need for, and likelihood of, continued affirmative action?

.......................................................................................................................................

.......................................................................................................................................

.......................................................................................................................................

.......................................................................................................................................

.......................................................................................................................................

# The 'American Dream'

The American Dream is that dream of a land in which life should be better and richer and fuller for everyone, with opportunity for each according to ability or achievement.

> The concept of 'the American Dream' is at the heart of American culture: the idea that one's prospects in life are determined by ability and energy rather than by family wealth or political connections. However, even since the end of formal segregation in 1965, it is questionable whether the American Dream realistically extends to African Americans.
>
> James Truslow Adams, *The Epic of America*, 1931

**6** Consider the observations on American society in the box below and what they might indicate about the 'American Dream' and American society generally.

1  There are many highly successful black Americans — for example Barack Obama, Condoleezza Rice, Colin Powell, Oprah Winfrey, Tiger Woods, Clarence Thomas.
2  Blacks remain twice as likely to be unemployed, three times as likely to live in poverty and more than six times as likely to be imprisoned relative to whites.
3  Obama failed to attract the majority of white votes in 2008.
4  Many feel that the federal government's slow response to the Hurricane Katrina catastrophe in 2005 was due to the fact that it was mainly poor black communities that were affected.
5  White and black Americans invariably attend different churches.
6  Due largely to 'white flight' to the suburbs, many school districts are now more racially segregated than they were 30 years ago.
7  Bill Cosby — a famous black comedian — made a speech in 2005 claiming that the black community largely had itself to blame for its relatively disadvantaged economic position.
8  Many minority groups, for example Jews, Italian-Americans and Asians, have done well economically in America.

9   Thirteen American states take away for life the right to vote of convicted felons. This disproportionately disenfranchises blacks: 13% of all black men have lost the right to vote in this way.

10  The majority of 'race hate' crimes in America now involve blacks and Hispanics.

11  When asked if his daughters should be able to benefit from affirmative action when they apply to college, President Obama remarked that: 'They should probably be treated by any admissions officer as folks who are pretty advantaged.'

a For each statement above, suggest what it appears to say about racial divisions in modern America.

## Extension question

b Where appropriate, evaluate your interpretation.

1

2

3

4

5

6

**7**

........................................................................................

........................................................................................

**8**

........................................................................................

........................................................................................

**9**

........................................................................................

........................................................................................

**10**

........................................................................................

........................................................................................

**11**

........................................................................................

........................................................................................

# Guided essay

Using the subheadings and notes provided below, write an essay plan for the following question:

**Why has affirmative action attracted growing criticism in the USA?**

(Try to provide up-to-date examples to support each point of analysis.)

## Introduction

Definition of affirmative action. Recognition of why it was introduced. Recognition of some of the main areas in which it was introduced.

........................................................................................

........................................................................................

........................................................................................

........................................................................................

........................................................................................

........................................................................................

## Evidence that AA action has become less popular

Shift in government priorities

'Negative' Supreme Court rulings

Decisions of state initiatives

*But* note that the Supreme Court, and society as a whole, seems to remain divided over the issue. NB: some recent state initiatives have decided to retain AA programmes (for example Colorado, 2008).

## Reasons why AA has become less popular

NB: try to distinguish between reasons why some people always opposed AA, and reasons why there is *growing* criticism.

It has done its job and is no longer needed.

It has proven not to work. NB: note the contradiction of these two arguments — which identifies the difficulty in assessing the 'success' of AA, since it involves hypothesising what would have happened in its absence.

It has proven to provide a disincentive to black communities.

It has meant that the best educational and employment opportunities have not been going to the best people, which has held back the American economy and American society.

Poverty is now spread across all communities — not just black communities.

There is a burgeoning black middle class that does not need AA assistance.

Many highly successful black individuals have shown that AA is not necessary to ensure the success of African Americans.

Other issues

......................................................................................................................

......................................................................................................................

......................................................................................................................

......................................................................................................................

## Conclusion

Since this question is asking you essentially for a one-sided argument rather than to evaluate
two sides of an argument, it is a good idea to try to qualify the statement as part of your
conclusion, i.e. by questioning whether AA has attracted 'growing' criticism, by pointing out
that there was always widespread opposition among conservatives, and that many sections of
society still appear divided over the issue.

......................................................................................................................

......................................................................................................................

......................................................................................................................

......................................................................................................................

......................................................................................................................

......................................................................................................................

......................................................................................................................

......................................................................................................................

......................................................................................................................